CONTROL ABILITY FOR YOU

Your Guide to Everything

A Traveler's Guide to Coping with the Universe and All That It Is—YOU!

Meaning-Control-Wisdom

ROBERT BELLINO M.D.

Fulton Books
Meadville, PA

Published by Fulton Books 2024

ISBN 979-8-88982-959-1 (paperback)
ISBN 979-8-88982-960-7 (digital)

Printed in the United States of America

PREFACE

This is a book about the meaning of life. It's also a book about you becoming everything that you can be. This means dealing with and controlling yourself and your thoughts so that you can experience life in a controlled, satisfied, and meaningful way. You can learn to realize, accept, and be the center of everything that is. Meaning, control, and wisdom are the desired and sought-after understandings of this book.

How to read this book: Each section is trying to get you to realize and use the truth that you are and only you are. To do that, you must read each list of words, phrases, and sentences after each introduction. Read and concentrate on them, each one again and again, until one or some have particular meaning to you. There are hundreds of statements, so you have a journey. But the most important is to repeat the words until you find some that you understand and then focus on them.

> God offers to every mind its choice between truth and repose. Take which you please—you can never have both. Between these as a pendulum, man oscillates ever. He in whom the love of repose predominates will accept the first creed, the first philosophy, the first philosophical party he meets—most likely his father's. He gets rest, commodity, and reputation; but he shuts the door of truth. He in whom the love of truth predominates will keep himself aloof from all moorings afloat. He will abstain from dogmatism, and recognize all the opposite negations between

which, as walls, his being is swung. He submits
to the inconvenience of suspense and imperfect
opinion; but he is a candidate for truth, as other
is not, and respects the highest law of his being.
(Ralph Waldo Emerson)

CHAPTER 1

Keep Going, Boy!

Look for a short positive word of wisdom in a book, in yourself, on YouTube,[*] or on any website. You must keep looking, understanding, and repeating all the short ways of thinking. In this book, you will find positive short sentences, words, or phrases to study, understand, and accept. Repeat them and find some or one that has meaning for you. Repeat it. Think about it. Concentrate on it. I start off with this because we are on a journey using our minds to find satisfaction and peace for a few seconds or a few hours. It is the same effect one gets from illicit drugs or liquor, but what you are looking for is not addictive and has no limits as you continue with it. In a book or on the computer, find these statements, repeat them, repeat them, repeat them all, and you will soon find one that is particularly satisfying for you. You must do this daily and more from now until the end. Always search for the wisdom that makes you strong personally—search and search, looking and looking, ending and unending. When you fail, start again, and again, and again, and you can find apples of gold. You will find wisdom, courage, and strength to continue the journey. Here are some statements that give us strength to continue in our resolve. Read them several times. Do you under-

---

[*] Go to YouTube or search the internet for wise sayings, or go to a store and buy a book about wise sayings.

stand? Does it refer to you? Write some of them down and keep them in your pocket…read them sometimes. Keep going, boy.

Happiness is possible only when one is busy. The body must toil; the mind must be occupied; and the heart must be satisfied. Those who do good as opportunity offers are sowing seeds all the time, and they need not doubt the harvest.

He who would have nothing to do with thorns
     must never attempt to gather flowers.
Every man's work is a portrait of himself.
All sunshine makes a desert.
All the flowers of tomorrow are in the seeds of today.
Today is the tomorrow you worried about yesterday.
Success is getting what you want; happiness is
     wanting what you get.
It isn't the load that weighs us down; it's the way we
     carry it.
Life is not the wick or the candle—it's the burning.
Wisdom consists in knowing what to do with
     what you know.
We do not see things as they are, but as we are.

Love not sleep, lest you come to poverty; open your eyes, and you will have plenty of bread.

—Proverbs 20:13

It is the glory of God to conceal things, but the glory of kings to search things out.

—Proverbs 25:2

CHAPTER 2

You Catch More Flies with Honey

People can get upset or angry when you say something angrily to them, or even when you say something to them pleasantly, positively, or modestly. They can get angry a little or a lot. You are much more likely to get a neutral or positive response when you say something neutral or positive. The question is, "What is being positive or neutral? Because most of us believe we know which is which, but we really don't." What then? It's a numbers game. When I say or do something, will I get an angry, neutral, or positive response?

No matter who you're talking to or performing for in some way, always talk neutrally or positively, recognizing that no matter what, sometimes you will get some form or amount of anger back. Your response to them is most important because that shows the world who is in control. Therefore, most importantly, it shows that you are in control of yourself. You and they may, should, would, and will demonstrate your power over yourself and magnificently over it and them. That is why you will catch more flies…

One sidenote: Be careful because things don't come out as we or they wish, but you have a plan that can satisfy you and make you successful. Remember, you are the center of the universe. You determine and define the past, the present, and the future. You catch more flies with honey than with vinegar. That is meant for you as well as them.

C H A P T E R 3

Nothing Is Good or Bad, but Thinking Makes It So

It has been said before that you yourself determine what is happy or sad, good or bad, up or down, and chaos or calm. This is about your control over yourself. You have total control over everyone and everything in the world with your mind because you determine what is happening, and this is about controlling the good and bad about you! Kings and dictators, they say, have controlled great numbers of countries since the beginning, but I am saying you control the ant, the horse, the planet, the universe, and whatever else there is out there. To reiterate, you determine how, what, why, when, and where everything known and unknown is; your thoughts and feelings make everything. To say it again, you make everything—feelings and things. Of course, the real secret is that very few know that or use that idea to create a better world inside and outside.

What can I do to get you to agree, accept, and use your power to change yourself and that is what will change the world? Recite the title of this chapter ten times a day for the next thirty days. It may do something. If it doesn't, then do it again and again. When you accept it, you will be able to change something for a period of time.

It's how you see things. You alone can change things, and it is in your mind. Think of yourself and try to change something that is upsetting, stressful, fearful, or scary. Change it into something that

4

is safe, comforting, and serene. You have the ability—maybe for two minutes or two seconds—but you can do it. If I can, then you can. When you do, you can extend the time and bring yourself some comfort. And bring to yourself some moral and mindful comfort.

This is a book about changing everything. This is a book about changing yourself. You are everything.

> Reason is the beginning of every work, and counsel precedes every understanding. As a clue to changes of heart four turns of fortune approach. Good and evil, life and death; and it has been the tongue that continually rules them. (Sirach 37:16–18 Revised Standard Version of Bible, Second Catholic Edition)

CHAPTER 4

Life Is a Valley of Tears

If things are always neutral or good, we will not be having this discussion, but things are usually neutral or bad. We have to define good, bad, and neutral for ourselves because you and I, as individuals, determine that. It places you at the center of the universe. Being conscious, therefore, places you at the center of everything because your thinking makes everything real for you. Then you determine the good, bad, up, down, dark, and light of everything. As you see and know, our feelings and interpretations of the world are often negative, and that negativity leads to all the discomfort, pain, fear, stress, anger, and negativity. That is brought about by our knowledge, interpretation, view, and varied feelings about life. For most of us (really all), we suffer because of the way we view ourselves, the world, reality, or others. So life is a valley of tears because we see it as such. There has to be a different life, one of happiness or satisfaction, to compare it with. Yes, for everything that is worldly has two parts: one plus and one minus, one up and one down, one good and one bad. Hallelujah! You can choose good or bad, love or hate, and then experience the effect of that choice, and it's only for you.

C H A P T E R 5

We All Like to Feel Good

Desiring to feel good is true for every one of us. But trying to define good is impossible. There is an experience of good from infancy—"see how satisfied the baby looks"—continued to the oldest of the aged, since everyone is personal in their definition and experience of the good, in which we seek ways of feeling. We seek ways of feeling good: eating, drinking, smoking marijuana, walking, sex, watching TV, bathing, and a myriad of other ways. Each one of us has, but it may not be for you. I cannot experience what you do, but I, like you, want to feel good. But only I can experience the good in myself. And only you can experience good in yourself; on its own, it cannot be described, although the experience can be different for you at different times. We see goodness or badness in others, and we feel it in ourselves. But trying to define it or describe it won't work. But it is an experience!

Describing feelings, good or bad, is difficult to impossible. Expressing feelings is something we do all the time. In others, it's rather simple—good, bad, happy, sad, angry, or calm—but in ourselves, we just generalize. All of us are generally not sure of the extent of our feelings, whatever they are.

But we all want to feel good, and we try to find ways to achieve it.

CHAPTER 6

Hey, You!

Yes, you! Trying to get someone's attention, or even our own, can be difficult or even impossible at times. You have to get your own attention to do something particularly for yourself, but how do we get our attention to do it with all the cacophony or discordant thoughts that come to us? We have to find a way to stop and then organize our thinking. Good idea? But how? We need to get our own attention, but there are ways to do that, and we have to do it. Maybe drinking a cold drink, scratching an itch, listening to loud music, focusing on a TV station you like, reading a love poem, or just saying "Stop it." Then for a moment when nothing is in your mind, say, "Hey, you! Who, me? Yes, you!" If you can say that you have gotten your attention for a second or even longer, then that is the beginning of you getting control of yourself and getting your own attention.

Recognize that anything we do to keep going, like remembering our beliefs and using or accepting them, requires time, practice, and work. And this time in your mind. Hey, you! Who, me? Yes, you!

CHAPTER 7

Strike while the Iron's Hot

The above title means to do something when you have the interest, ability, and strength to do it. Everything that has been said so far is a journey. It requires you and everything else. Remember that you are the center, and everything else is outside of you and depends on how you think about it. Yes, you! I hope you can begin to realize how important you are to yourself and everything else because you determine your thinking, feelings, features, and existence. You have the ability to change everything outside and inside yourself.

Attention to something is what makes or breaks its existence. Developing the resources to think properly about anything is in you, requires you, and is you. Recognition comes from reaching the source, but it requires action, investment, practice, and stamina. But I can say that it is everyone's ability, but it must be done at the proper time, with the proper thought, and with recognition that you decide everything in your mind and have the ability to change these thoughts so that you may have a modicum of serenity with peace, thinking with acceptance, and knowing that you started when you had the knowledge, ability, and strength to do it. You can "strike while the iron is hot!" and realize your own control.

CHAPTER 8

Use Both Your Legs

Everything said so far is about the world, your mind, you and them, and yours and theirs. But the most important report is about the spiritual side of the existence of God. He has done everything—before, during, and after. He tells us that he will help us through this valley of tears. But He still absolutely gives us the power to change things, so we must first accept God as ALL and ask Him to help us in our journey through life, where you are beginning to get control over our thinking and feelings, but God is everything.

This is about a change in the direction of your thinking. You do have control over your thinking to a degree, but worldly circumstances and God's involvement are evident. This is a discourse on getting control of your thoughts by using your own control, ability, and interests. But remember, God is everything, everything, and everything. And I know that when you accept that, it gives you some control over your thinking, feelings, and behavior. Yet it is a journey, not a blip.

So now we must go full force, asking God to help us change our thoughts, feelings, experiences, and behaviors in the "valley of tears." God told us to pray like this:

The Lord's Prayer

Our father who art in Heaven
Hallowed be thy name
Thy Kingdom come
Thy will be done on earth as it is in heaven.
Give us this day our daily bread
Forgive us our debts
As we forgive our debtors
And lead us not into temptation
But deliver us from evil.
For thine is the kingdom and the power and the
    glory. Forever.
Amen.

Also:

Happy moments, praise God
Difficult moments, seek God
Quiet moments, worship God
Painful moments, trust God
Every moment, thank God

Using both your mental and spiritual legs in life gives you the tools, resources, reality, power, and truth to find a modicum of serenity, tranquility, and peace. It is a journey, and if you accept it, even to some degree, what was said about control and how to find it is yours. The other way of doing it (your way) is too dangerous, destructive, degrading, and easy, and the outcome is too ominous. But the journey we discussed here can lead to tranquility and peace, leading to power. Remember that control and positive thinking and feelings are not necessarily continuous. But because you can find it, or them, through reading and studying for a second or an hour, you realize that you can do it with this described meditation. You can have it longer and more often throughout your life. Pray, pray, think, think, experience, experience, live, live, feel good, feel good, and LOVE, LOVE because God is Love. Know the meaning of life! You and God! God!

CHAPTER 9

Meaning

One of the things we can do is find meaning in suffering. From the beginning, turn to God and ask, beg, and beseech Him. That is prayer, no matter how you do it. The intensity of your prayer is very important—not for God but for you. If you do that continually, you will find what you are looking for, but maybe have not defined, sooner or later, mildly or intensely. This is a book about finding the way, believing it can be done, and doing it for yourself. The only absolute in the discourse is "You can do it!"

You could or should go after the meaning in your life. Search for it, though it may vary. For many, it basically means purpose, and there are infinite purposes and therefore meanings. Only you can find those for yourself. You are the center of everything. You see everything going on, but only you can give it meaning. Others can have meaning in themselves, but you can't experience it. So your job is to find meaning that will release or reduce the negative feelings in yourself. It is the attitude you take about making that change in you, not in them or it. A positive attitude, when produced, may lessen pain. It starts or increases any pleasure, reduces disappointment, and increases satisfaction and happiness.

Remember, you decide for yourself while experiencing good or bad, pleasant or unpleasant, helpful or bad, meaning for yourself or nonsense. The most important thing is to realize that you are the patient and therapist in discovering what you are like. What you are.

Some of these statements can be applied to yourself sooner or later. Others, you can understand and become them from a small amount to a large amount.

Find what you should be, can be, and are:

Joy
Gratitude
Interest
Serenity
Hope
Fun time
Inspiration
Forgiveness
Ambition
Intelligence
Timeless
LOVE
love

Now here are more thoughts about finding yourself. All apply to you.

Evaluate, not judge.
Reason
Assign things to yourself, not others.
Open
Point to something positive in your mind or your mood.
Put it into action.
Triumph
Master it
Courage
Begin now
Truth
Multiply it
Present it
Patience

You can know yourself.
Self-realization
Reflect
Wholeness
Best enemy
Permanency
Eternity
The pinnacle
Self—yourself
Further-looking, reaching, seeking, demanding
Generalization
Palpable
Seek
New consciousness
Let the seed germinate.
Fulfillment
Validation
Function
Fearless
Defense
Internal things—feelings and thoughts
Abilities
Safety
Possibility and understanding
The control of yourself can be found in you with your effort.
Reality
Everything is now.
Being is now
Focus on the here and now.
Experience

If you don't know what some of these words mean, look them up in a dictionary, and the meaning is there for you. Read each word, phrase, or sentence and ask, *What does this mean, and what does this have to do with me?* Recognize that you and so many others have asked this question, and many have not gotten the answers because they stopped thinking about it too soon. The answers to the questions will help you recognize that you are the center of everything that is and will be, and you can change. The center becomes something controlled, satisfying, and also productive for the whole world since you can change into something controlled. You are worldly and spiritual. Use worldly ability and expression to be spiritual, which is everything, forever. The question is, would you and your mind cease to be if you stopped thinking, or would you cease to be if your body died? But there is a difference between the body and the mind because the mind is there and the body isn't after a short while. Are you searching for something you already have?

CHAPTER 10

What?

The best victory is to conquer yourself. Nice thinking if you can do it! This is a study proposing that you, by yourself, can change using your mind; you can change anything and everything, anywhere, anytime, by changing yourself, and the change is completely in yourself. The following is a list of things you can do, accept, appreciate, and make part of your existence. These are all positive thoughts. Repeating these statements again and again, and still again and again, can make them reality for you alone. The true meaning for you. Some of these statements, phrases, or sentences may not make sense to you. Repeat reading them, and then go on. Certain statements will have meaning for you, and that's why you must go to each one and focus on each one. Mark the ones that have meaning for you and go on. Most things have an opposite. These statements do too, but don't go there. Going there could be painful, stressful, and negative to the nth degree. That is why I say to focus on the positive, the real, and the healing words given here. The following are words, statements, questions, suggestions, and commands:

Self-control
Restraint of behavior and thoughts
Healthy habits
Striving
Inner peace for short or long periods

Intuition or mental view
Take responsibility.
Forgiveness, especially for yourself
Empathy for everything or just one thing
Cultivating goals
Focus on your thinking.
Live for something.
Believing in your ability
Knowing that you can change your thinking or the thinking
Optimism for yourself
Humor
Resolve it or not.
Pride, yes, pride
Positive thinking
Freedom to feel
Freedom to think
Freedom to change thinking
Seeking advice and guidance within yourself
Choose.
Make decisions.
Let yourself do it.
Understanding worry
Think about your attitude.
Think about your potential.
Recognize that it could be worse.
Transcendence or beyond limits, extraordinary
Man is more than a psyche, or mind.
Anticipating stress is called worry.
Thinking
Feeling
Behavior
Live by and live for meaningfulness.
Will
Gratefulness
Great
Be great

Value
Courageous deeds
Believe and know that you are forever.
In therapy, believe your therapist is kind, safe, interested,
strange, caring, positive, knowledgeable, and understanding.
Imagine
Encounter
Trust yourself
love—Love
Attitude
Change is all you.
Why?
Power to do anything small or large for a short time or longer
Grow
Go
Obtain salvation.
Awaken
Control yourself.
Everything is yours.
Pay attention
You are reality.
Slow down, speed up, and change.
Certainty
Small things can be made large.
Large things can be made small.
Persistence
Persistently practice
Learn from success and failure.
Create
Answers to your questions
Willingness
Decide
Voluntary thinking
Pursue
Being
Mindfulness

Sense of self
What you think about is what you feel.
Look at the future.
Look at the present.
Look at the past.
Time or timeless
Purpose
React in a positive way.
Deep thinking
Thinking about your thoughts
Looking at and seeing things differently
Unstuck
God

Ask and it will be given to you, seek and ye shall find; Knock and it will be open to you. For everyone who asks receives, and the one who seeks finds and to the one who knocks it will be opened. (Matthew 7:7–8)

Chapter 11

Wisdom

Coming this far, you have wisdom, defined by Wikipedia as "the ability to contemplate and act productively using knowledge, experience, understanding, common sense, and insight. Wisdom is associated with attributes such as unbiased judgment, compassion, experiential self-knowledge, self-transcendence, and nonattachment." That's you! Maybe a little or maybe a lot, but still there. That makes you special in your ability to understand being and to be.

What is the greatest good?
Are you enlightened yet?
Only you
What is the most important thing? Past, future, or now?
***How* is more important than *what* and *they* depends on an *I*.**
Action, some action, no action
Attached, partially attached, detached
You are, no matter what you think.
Are you being tested?
Witnessing your thoughts and emotions
is the beginning of freedom.
Special words that are more than their definition
or meaning: Repeat, repeat, repeat.
Healing, redemption, love, acceptance,
surrender, happiness—now.

Are you a prisoner, a spectator, or a doer?
Is said better than unsaid?
Is unsaid better than said?

The following are mind strategies. It is not about where, why, or when, but how you do it. That is change.

Strength. Power, energy, thoughts, interests, courage, praises, searches, good deeds, your wisdom, your appetite for all things, your ability to rejoice, your knowledge, your sincerity, your appearance, your losses
Silence at the right moment
What if?
Your now
Memory
Life situations
Goal setting
Coping
Your recipes
Circumstances
Experiences
Present moment
Waiting
Present
Consciousness
Satisfaction
Happiness
Attention
Reaction
Desire
Acceptance
Self
Your truth
Your self-trust

The "*how*" you change is about you realizing that you can do it, that you are the only one who can change, and that you are the center of everything. Up until now, the center has been distressing, but reading and discovering things about yourself give you the power to make the change. "The outer purpose belongs to the horizontal dimensions of space and time; the inner purpose concerns a deepening of your being in the vertical dimension of timeless now" (Eckhart Tolle).

There is a gap between perceiving something and thinking about it. The narrower the space, the more intense the emotion coming from it. It's like a door slamming in your face or slowly closing in front of you. The longer you have, the better you can deal with perceptions and think about them. So slow down when thinking about things. After having knowledge about, thinking about, receiving an impression of, or knowing something, slow down in thinking about it. In this way, the original thought will stress you much less than a door slamming in your face. Bam!

Change is a variation, and as you know, it is good or bad, and it is putting one thing in place of another. But that can be a problem since we don't always know one thing from another, like saying "to change horses." Our problem is that we don't usually know when, where, or how. We may also not know what the horse is. Change, then, is to unfold, make something known, lay open, and even discover. It's a journey with repetitions, tiredness, fears, and confusion about how to change. But keep going because you are the center. You decide what was, is, and will be because you are.

You define wisdom for yourself, but you have it small or large because you are trying to understand life—past, present, and future. You can make your wisdom increase by continuing on the task you have before you, which is reflections on critical thinking and transcendental judgment of being, which means to get and have mindful and spiritual understanding.

CHAPTER 12

Awareness

Again, how do you use this book? It may take you hours, days, or years, but keep doing it. Read some words, phrases, or sentences, and maybe you will find some that strike a chord with you. Now not a negative one because you and I are trying to find positive, true, and enlightening things about you. We don't deny negativity, especially negative thoughts and feelings. But we are going on to find out who we are, what we are, when we are, and why we are. Take the words you read as eternal wisdom for you. Again, to reiterate, let what you read here be good, honorable, and loving for you since you are capable, able, and everything.

You have access to your being. You are the center of yourself—of everything that was, is, and will be. You experience everything before, during, or after—strong or weak, true or not, good or bad. You are enlightened. It is not only that you define the words and phrases herein but that you observe the feelings coming from them and then, with time, understand and experience them. Attention is then the first step in understanding, accepting, and living life.

Imprisoned in your mind?
Perception vs. thought
Don't get attached to words.
Attached to understanding
Control

Freedom
Laugh
Presences
Does time exist?
Silence
Body, mind, and something else
Connection—unconnect, disconnect, reconnect, misconnect
Point to or from reality
Is your mind working for you?
Can you observe your mind…? Impossible?
Believe and/or know
Value
Being is more than mind.
Reality
Seeker and/or finder
Surprised?
Fascinating or enlightening
Fascinating, enlightening, or liberating
Formlessness
Innovator
Impress
Peace
Observe
Visible and invisible—seen and unseen
Request, demand, or question
One with all
Luminous thoughts
Think about feelings.
Feeling vs. thinking
Mental vs. emotional
Drawing your attention
Think or listen.
The or a portal
Search
Inner silence vs. outer silence
Recognize and realize your gifts as special attributes.

Pilgrimage
Abundance
Fulfillment
Liberated
God

"Death shall be no more. Neither shall there be morning, crying, nor pain anymore, for the former things have passed away" (Rev. 21:4).

Do you act, or do you react?
Do you control, or do you not control?
Control—in, is, are, might, could, may, should, would
Existential plenty instead of existential emptiness, or a vacuum?
Become aware of possibilities.
Advise yourself.

The loss of self-esteem comes from negativism. All the above and those coming words, phrases, and sentences are a means of reducing or stopping low self-esteem. But you must find the ones that are for you alone, repeat them, think about them, experience them, define them, and be them.

You can inherit a grand future right now. Go after it with all your might. Meaning is fullness. Fullness is meaning. Do you have a purpose? No? Why not? What's the difference between having and not having a purpose?

The following are from the epilogue of *The Power of Positive Living* by Norman Vincent Peale:

1. How to be turned on to a joy-packed lifestyle
2. How to be a positive thinker
3. How to really believe in yourself
4. Ways to drop the "I can't" reaction
5. Believe that happiness is always possible.
6. When things look bad, remember the word "but."
7. Affirm faith, the great enemy of fear.

8. Always remember the healing power of your mind.
9. Remember, you have comeback power.
10. The secret of success is uncomplicated and possible.
11. Practice the positive power of believing.
12. No need to feel empty—get full of the power of faith.
13. Be an asset to yourself.
14. You have a censor. It pays to heed it.
15. Get the fire of enthusiasm burning and keep it going always.

CHAPTER 13

Acceptance

The following is what you can be by learning what you should be and are:

Depth

Balance vs. out of balance

Silence needs sound, and sound needs silence.

Nothing could be without space around it, which
is nothing but what you can conceive.

The luminous splendor of the colorless light of
emptiness *(Tibetan Book of the Dead)*

Are you something?

What is your purpose?

Do you have time?

Realize, recognize, and get there because you are free now.

Stop looking to the future or the past. You are now.

Liberation

How does one get a sense of who he or she is?

Do all the negative hopes, feelings,
expectations, and needs still exist?

You can become a watcher instead of an experiencer.

You are not only mind but so much more right now.

Is what you do a force of habit?

Freedom comes with time; time comes with freedom.

This is a challenge for only you.
Doesn't God know everything about you? Then he
knows you're reading this discourse about
everything…God.
Self-determination
Personal
Some things are unavoidable. Remove it or them!
Attitude is the beginning of changing anything.
Hold your head up high.
Negative positivism vs. optimistic pessimism

So for all the previous things, it is simple. You become what you think, but you are more than thinking.

Can one be right or wrong at the same time?
The ego is not the complete you.
Are you a student and/or a teacher?
Does good really have an opposite?
When things change within, they also change without.
When things change without, they do not have to change within.
Your life story is not all about you.
Transformation
Is up good and down bad?
Is up bad and down good?
Every experience has its opposite. If not,
there would be no experience.
Can or do emotions send messages to us?
Compassion for yourself and others is a
combination of joy and sadness.
Odd? Or even? You decide.
Loyalty to yourself
Advise yourself properly.
Quality
Heal, healing, and healer
Depth
Balance vs. out of balance

Silence needs sound, and sound needs silence.
Nothing could be without space around it, which
is nothing but what you can conceive.
Are you something?
What is your purpose?
Do you have time?
Realize, recognize, and get there because you are free now.
Stop looking to the future or the past. You are now.
Victory
Constructive
Energy
You determine
Self-permission
Direct action
Persistence
Practice
Attain
Self-confidence
Refuse the inferiority and superiority complexes.
You do it.
Refuse and refute inferiority feelings, lack
of confidence, and self-doubt.
Valuable feelings, worthless feelings
Valuable thoughts and worthless thoughts
Valuable behavior, worthless behavior
Decide.
Good patterns
Negative thoughts, dangerous thoughts
Negative feelings, dangerous feelings
Negative behavior, dangerous behavior
God is with me.
Safety
Have and use positive thoughts.
Defining a word or concept demands that
you know the opposite, or does it?
Remember and/or forget.

"Better is a handful of quietness that two hands full
of toil and a striving after wind." (Ecclesiastes
4:6)
You influence yourself.
Accelerate—decelerate
Inner peace
"What is your lot in life?" (Ecclesiastes 5:18)
"If thou canst believe, all things are possible
to him that believe it." (Mark 9:23)
Learn to expect the best, not the worst.
Think of positive possibilities—will, might, maybe, and could.
Thought patterns: Can you change them?
Energy, effort, ability—you
A driving force to believe, know, create, and possess
Insight
Have a goal, the goal, goals.
Thinking changes everything.
Positive expectations
Assurance
Dynamic spiritual thinking
Is there anything you can do about it?
What's your mental attitude?
Tune in, on, or out.
Is your thinking habitual or new?
What was it yesterday?
What will it be tomorrow?
Take control.
What should I do if little or nothing changes? GOD!
New ideas in your mind
Brand-new ideas in your mind
Can you carry a mustard seed in your pocket?
Surrender yourself to the restorative powers of God.

Do you believe that the causes of ill health and other stress can
be anger, hate, irritation, fear, worry, insecurity, negative thinking, a
poor attitude, a lack of trust, being controlled by yourself or others,

unwillingness, worldliness, a lack of purpose, attachment thinking, difference, thinking you are nothing, weak, or without purpose or freedom? Now you decide: What are you? Know that you can change it. Do it!

There has been some neglect by psychotherapists and others in explaining and telling people about their own ability to know and change themselves in mind, body, and thinking. This means their being… How is that done? This way is to read words, phrases, and sentences that will give you the means and tools to change anything and everything. At its base is positive thinking, but you must find and choose the best words for you. Those you can understand, accept, and like! To reiterate, you are the center of the universe—the center of everything. You determine what everything is. You can change absolutely everything, but that is a journey that you have started since you are reading this book.

As you think, so it shall be. In my opinion, a very good way to change, feel positive, and be successful in yourself is to read chapter 13 of the book *The Power of Positive Thinking* by Norman Vincent Peale. That is a chapter on why, how, and what to do with regard to positive change in you.

Curative trust in God
A sound philosophy
A satisfying philosophy
Live or act differently.
Indestructibility! Or?
Charged, supercharged, uncharged, and undercharged
Gainsay or yes
Is there a higher power? Use it!
Think differently.
Thinking creates thoughts.
Thoughts create thinking.
Creative idea?
Certainty or indubitableness, or give in to doubt?
Spiritualize?
Unspiritualize

Interior life or exterior life?
Understanding and applying
How does one get there?
Live free.
Mundane or ordinary?
Spiritual or extraordinary
Inner change
An answer
A new answer, the answer
Yourself, itself, a self, the self! You.
Transformation
Can we get away from time?
Could there be a now without time?
Now!
"Self-control and prudence, justice and courage; nothing
is more profitable for men than these." (Wisdom 8:7)
Connectedness
Liberation and/or freedom
In the world, thoughts are sometimes; feelings are all the time.
Feelings and thoughts are only part of you.
Salvation
Desire, desirous
Experience it or watch it.
Watch it, be taken over by it, or stop it.
Pureness
Eternal
Beyond
Realize truth.
Watcher or experiencer
"It is the glory of God to conceal things, but the glory
of kings to search things out." (Proverbs 25:2)

Coming this far again, you have wisdom defined by Wikipedia as "the ability to contemplate and act productively using knowledge, experience, understanding, common sense, and insight. Wisdom is associated with attributes such as unbiased judgment, compassion, experiential self-knowledge, self-transcendence, and nonattachment." That's you! Maybe a little or maybe a lot, but still there. That makes you special in your ability to understand being and to be. You define wisdom for yourself, and you have it small or large because you are trying to understand life—past, present, and future. You can make your wisdom increase by continuing on the task before you, which is reflection on continued thinking and transcendent judgment of being, which means to get and have mindful and spiritual understanding.

The words you read are information, but they can, through more understanding and repetition, draw you into a new understanding and consciousness that is both worldly and unworldly. And again, you do it and finally put all your attention on those words, phrases, and sentences that have meaning to you now! Have a real state of existence! **BE**!

About the Author

Dr. Robert J. Bellino
Psychiatrist

Age: 88
Specialty: General Psychiatry
Practicing: 55 years
Retired: June 1, 2022

Personality

Dr. Bellino is a caring, interested, and aware professional psychiatrist with multiple experiences that make him an authority on dealing with life issues and emotional illness. He used psychotherapy and medication management to help many people cope with life for fifty-five years. Additionally, in his medical practice, Dr. Bellino employed various alternative techniques such as hypnosis, relaxation techniques, group therapy, couples' therapy, and individual therapy with psychotherapy and medication management. Dr. Bellino feels strongly that the relationship formed between doctor and patient is the most important aspect of treatment.

Health and Grooming

Dr. Bellino feels that it's important to stay active, eat well, and dress according to the situation or event. Each event or situation dictates what a participant wears. Attending a baseball game dictates sportswear. Attending a wedding dictates that the guests wear their finery. In his practice, Dr. Bellino wore a suit or coat and tie every day because he believes that you become what you think, and people will think differently about you if you have leisure clothes or dress clothes on. A bush with flowers is more impressive than the same bush with no flowers, but it is the same bush. Which bush are you? You can change.

About the Doctor

Dr. Bellino was a psychiatrist for fifty-five years. He is a member of Phi Beta Kappa. He graduated in the top third of his medical school class. He had three years of general psychiatry residency. In private practice, he used multiple kinds of psychiatric procedures, including shock treatment therapy, group therapy, hypnosis, and individual therapy lasting 25–60 minutes with medication management. He went to prisons, jails, nursing homes, and hospitals, and he managed and advised other therapists in hospitals and outpatient settings. Dr. Bellino saw over fifteen thousand different patients individually throughout his career.